Thoughts on Art & Artists

Words by Robert Brault

Artwork by Joan Brault

<> <> <>

~~~

*"To steal a moment from the sublime
and store it out of the reach of time
is given perhaps to angels and saints
and lowly dabblers in pencils and paints."*

~~~

"Kennebunkport Summer" - oil by Joan Brault

<> <> <>

"Fall Pond" - watercolor by Joan Brault

"Winter Blues" - oil by Joan Brault

<><><>

Writer's Note

I want to underscore the fact that all writings in this book are original.

Some may ring familiar, having appeared on the internet and in media outlets around the world. Over the years I've been pleased to see my thoughts quoted on more than a million internet sites.

It is difficult to protect one's creative rights to short writings such as these, and I am accustomed to seeing my items credited to others, often to the famous. My books are a hopeful attempt to lay claim to the major part of my work. That said, I do encourage the free, non-commercial use of my items, asking only attribution. I expect commercial users to contact me for permission.

Robert Brault
bobbrault@att.net
rbrault.blogspot.com

<><><>

Table of Contents

<><><>

<>‹›<>

Preface

You will notice that the book is laid out not in chapters or sections but in "galleries." This seemed a permissible quaintness in a book about art. You are invited to imagine yourself in a "thought museum," so to speak, each saying an exhibit on the wall of a gallery. The illusion is encouraged by presenting the exhibits one to a page. The hope is that you will pause in front of each, perhaps taking a moment to fold arms, stroke chin and thoughtfully critique. You are invited, if you wish, to discuss with other readers who might be browsing over your shoulder.

Each gallery caters to a quite different perspective. In Gallery One, "Dry, Sly and Wry," the author maintains the attitude of an amused onlooker. The tone is on the light side, a bit droll at times, as befits a commentator whose credentials might also be characterized as light and a bit droll.

In Gallery Two, however, all such reserve is thrown to the winds. Titled for a reason, "Let's Get Serious," the tone is weightier, more thoughtful, more replete with the subtle insights

<>‹›<>

of a practiced sideline observer. Edification may be found here, especially if one is not too precise in defining the word.

The mood shifts again in Gallery Three, "From The Cheering Section." Here we find a selection of encouragements taken from the commentator's earlier books. Although not written expressly for artists, their relevance to the artist's endeavor rings remarkably true, a credit, perhaps, to the universal applicability of encouragement.

Upon leaving the museum's Gallery Three, you are escorted into "The Outer Hall" where several personal vignettes are hung, and the book's authors await for a "meet and greet" of sorts. Alas, no refreshments are served.

As for the book's artwork, the artist presents her exhibits in the lobby, at the entrance and interior of each gallery and in the outer hall. Some relationship to theme is attempted but not rigorously held to, the objective being to provide an occasional breath of art as respite from the framed word.

That, then, is the book. Facetiousness aside, it is intended principally as an entertainment, but a few things are meant seriously, and, if the reader takes them seriously, the authors would be pleased. In all, the collection is offered as a small

<><><>

tribute to the talented and persevering individuals who comprise the artist's world -- a motley clan of all ages and genders, shapes and sizes -- in whose company the book's authors have shared many a glass and improved many an hour.

Robert Brault
Joan Brault
Avon, Connecticut
July 2021

A Note On Convention

In putting thoughts into words, the author-writer faced the dilemma of whether to use the 'he" or "she" pronoun in referring to the artist. The resolution was to alternate the two from item to item. Hopefully, this will not prove too disconcerting to the reader.

~~~

<><><>

<><><>

"Black Tulip," *mixed media by Joan Brault*

<></><>

Gallery One

Dry, Sly & Wry

~~~

The mind as you age
Is an artist, it seems.
Monet paints your mem'ries,
Picasso your dreams.

~~~

<></><>

<>< ><>

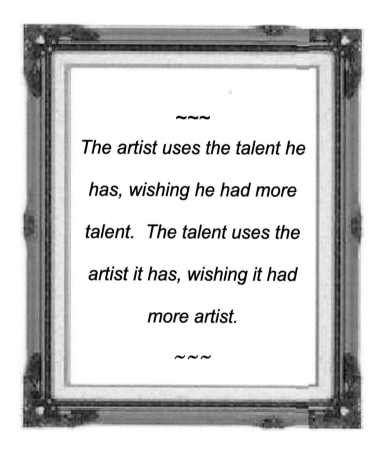

~~~

The artist uses the talent he has, wishing he had more talent. The talent uses the artist it has, wishing it had more artist.

~~~

<>< ><>

<><><>

~~~

Oh, how much simpler

art would be,

If eyes could paint

Or brush could see.

~~~

<><><>

<><><>

~~~

Every painting, no matter how

successful, leaves the artist

with another chance to paint

what she had in mind.

~~~

<><><>

<>><><>

~~~

A painting is what you make of it, besides which, "Moon Weeping" has a better ring to it than "Paintbrush Dripping."

~~~

<>><><>

<>< ><>

~~~

The artistic effort is a menage

a trois -- the artist, his muse

and his talent, the latter two

always running off and having

to be coaxed back.

~~~

<>< ><>

<>< ><>

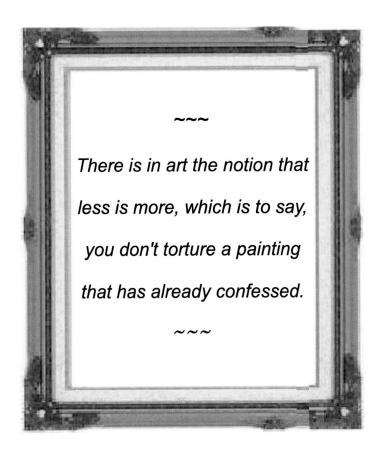

~~~

There is in art the notion that

less is more, which is to say,

you don't torture a painting

that has already confessed.

~~~

<>< ><>

~~~

Every work of art requires a

finishing touch, best applied

at the first inclination to do so.

~~~

<>< ><>

<>< ><>

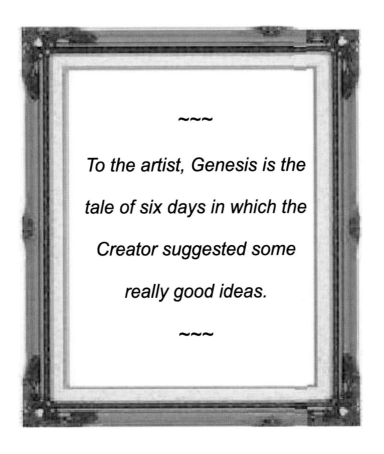

~~~

To the artist, Genesis is the tale of six days in which the Creator suggested some really good ideas.

~~~

<>< ><>

<>\<>\<>

"North Hero Sunset" - oil by Joan Brault

<>\<>\<>

<><><>

"Fishing at Galway" - pastel by Joan Brault

<><><>

<><><>

~~~

The first assumption of an art critic is that the artist meant to paint something else.

~~~

<><><>

<><><>

~~~

There are days when luring a subject into a frame can be as challenging as urging a 2-year-old thoroughbred into a starting gate.

~~~

<><><>

<><><>

~~~

The artist must marry her talent -- and the two must elope. A big church wedding is fatal.

~~~

<><><>

<><><>

~~~

On the one hand, don't let the perfect be the enemy of the good. On the other hand, recognize that the good has worse enemies.

~~~

<><><>

<>\<>\<>

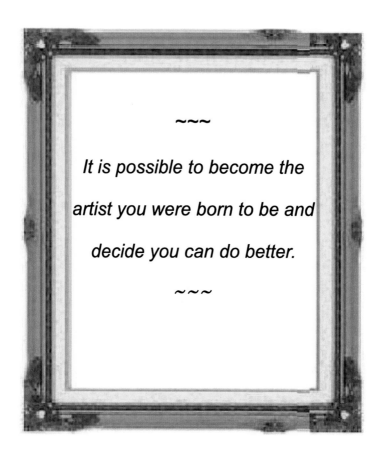

~~~

It is possible to become the artist you were born to be and decide you can do better.

~~~

<>\<>\<>

<>< ><>

~~~

The painter needs all the imagination of the poet, plus hand-eye coordination.

~~~

<>< ><>

<>< ><>

~~~

One unique thing about the artist's endeavor is that you never know if you're having a bad brush day or launching a new genre.

~~~

<>< ><>

<><><>

~~~

Some first efforts are such perfect disasters that there's nothing to do but sit back and admire their perfection.

~~~

<><><>

<><><>

"Still Life," pastel by Joan Brault

Gallery Two

Let's Get Serious

~~~

Only in sway
To an artist's will
Does life, for a moment,
Consent to be still.

~~~

<><><>

<>

~~~

That portion of reality that can

be composed within a frame

can be understood.

~~~

<>

<>< ><>

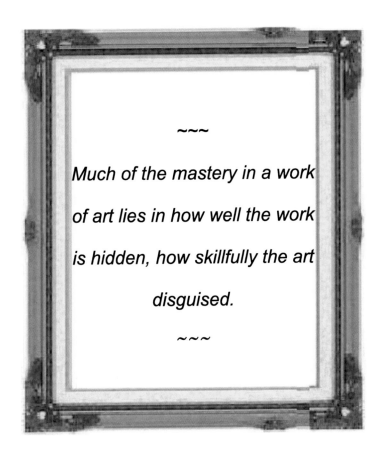

~~~

Much of the mastery in a work of art lies in how well the work is hidden, how skillfully the art disguised.

~~~

<>< ><>

<><><>

~~~

Perfection in art, as often in life, is better captured by eraser than pencil.

~~~

<><><>

<> <> <>

~~~

It is easier to reach perfection

than to stop there.

~~~

<> <> <>

<>＜><>

~~~

What you often see in a

lesser work of art is a subject

perfectly captured but never

set free.

~~~

<>＜><>

<>< ><>

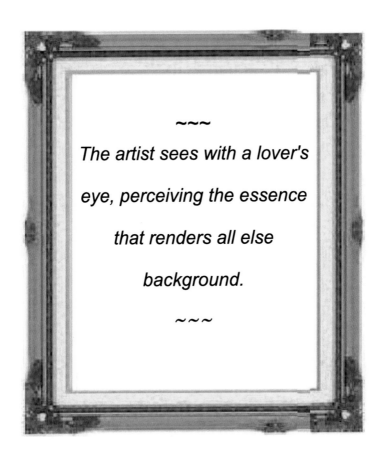

~~~

The artist sees with a lover's eye, perceiving the essence that renders all else background.

~~~

<>< ><>

<><><>

~~~

Every artist is influenced by others. Originality is as much in the blend of your influences as in the mix of your colors.

~~~

<><><>

<>‍<>‍<>

~~~

It's not about discovering your talent. It's about pushing your talent to the limit and discovering your genius.

~~~

<>‍<>‍<>

"Isle of Capri" - pastel by Joan Brault

<>‌<>‌<>

"Barn in Winter" - watercolor by Joan Brault

<>‌<>‌<>

<><><>

~~~

The artist's talent sits uneasy

as an object of public acclaim,

having so long been an object

of private despair.

~~~

<><><>

<><><>

~~~

Sometimes, to pursue a new idea, the artist must forfeit her deposit on an old idea.

~~~

<><><>

<> <> <>

~~~

Most of what we know of the human soul goes by the name of art appreciation.

~~~

<> <> <>

<><><>

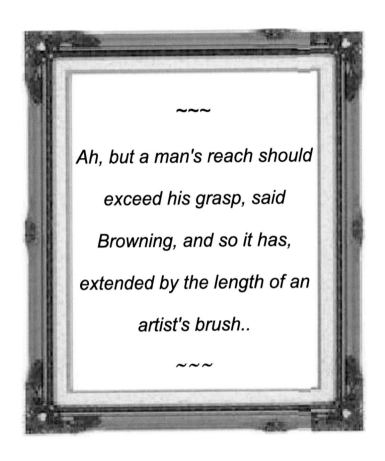

~~~

Ah, but a man's reach should

exceed his grasp, said

Browning, and so it has,

extended by the length of an

artist's brush..

~~~

<><><>

<>><><>

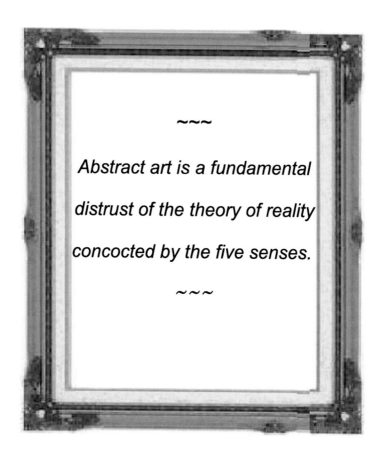

~~~

Abstract art is a fundamental

distrust of the theory of reality

concocted by the five senses.

~~~

<>< ><>

~~~

The problem with settling for good enough is that it's so hard to distinguish it from almost good enough.

~~~

<>< ><>

<>< ><>

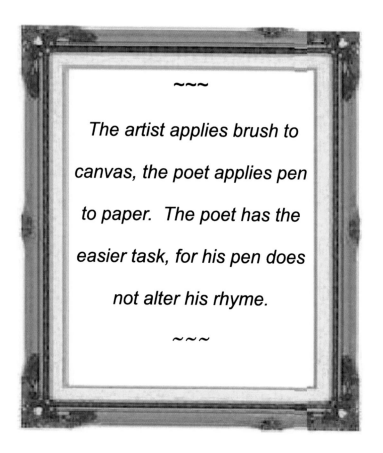

~~~

The artist applies brush to canvas, the poet applies pen to paper. The poet has the easier task, for his pen does not alter his rhyme.

~~~

<>< ><>

<>< ><>

~~~

Art is all about deciding what to maximize and what to minimize in order to maximize it.

~~~

<>< ><>

<><><>

"Flowers," watercolor by Joan Brault

Gallery Three

From The Cheering Section

~~~

Who painted the stars?
Who molded the hours?
Who sculpted the planets?
Who sent the flowers?

~~~

<><><>

~~~

A nod, a bow,
And a tip of the lid
To the person
Who coulda
And shoulda
And did!

~~~

<><><>

<><><>

~~~

Sometimes you feel like giving up, but then you look at others who have given up, and the results aren't that good.

~~~

<><><>

<>< ><>

~~~

We all have our limitations,

but when we listen to our

critics, we also have theirs.

~~~

<>< ><>

<><><>

~~~

Never be discouraged by the

opinion of people who don't

know what you're about to

accomplish.

~~~

<><><>

<> <> <>

~~~

Do not look to find your identity in some particular work. Look to stamp your identity on whatever work you do.

~~~

<> <> <>

<><><>

~~~

The road to success is not a

path you find but a trail you

blaze.

~~~

<><><>

<>< ><>

~~~

When it seems like something

can't be done, start it, and see

if the rest of it can be done.

~~~

<>< ><>

<><><>

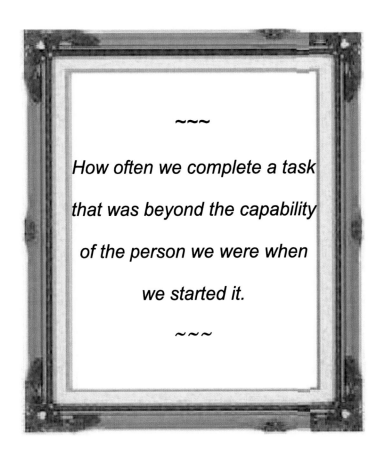

~~~

How often we complete a task

that was beyond the capability

of the person we were when

we started it.

~~~

<><><>

<><><>

"Ibis" - pastel by Joan Brault

<><><>

<>< ><>

"Jack" - oil by Joan Brault

<><><>

<>&<><>

~~~

You start making progress in life when you realize that you don't always have to resume where you left off.

~~~

<>&<><>

<>‹›<>

~~~

The thing to remember when everyone seems to doubt you is that everyone has not been born yet.

~~~

<>‹›<>

<> <> <>

~~~

The surest way to become the artist you are meant to be is to take it upon yourself to mean it.

~~~

<> <> <>

<><><>

~~~

It is better to be a first rate

you than a second rate

someone else, even if it costs

you a blue ribbon now and

then.

~~~

<><><>

<>< ><>

~~~

We find in ourselves the strength to overcome every obstacle -- a good thing, because we also find in ourselves every obstacle.

~~~

<>< ><>

<><><>

~~~

Every day spent happily striving toward an elusive goal is to achieve the real goal, which is to spend our days happily.

~~~

<><><>

<>< ><>

~~~

Yes, commitment requires

energy, but, fortunately, it is

the best known source of it.

~~~

<>< ><>

<>< ><>

~~~

Be always forgiving of the person you were -- and demanding of the person you wish to become.

~~~

<>< ><>

<> <> <>

"Just We Two," pastel by Joan Brault

<><><>

The Outer Hall

The Authors Go To Paris

A Stroll on the Champs

A Visit to the Louvre

A Visit to the Monet Gardens

A Writer's Reverie

~~~

Meet The Author

Meet The Artist

~~~

<><><>

The Authors Go To Paris

In the fall of 2008, Joan and I made our first and only visit to Paris. The focus of our visit was the Louvre, the home and gardens of Claude Monet at Giverny and the Impressionist exhibits at the Musee d'Orsay and the Tuileries. We stayed at a small hotel on the Left Bank and dined in restaurants and cafes in Saint Germain. Following are a few impressions of that visit.

~~~

<><><>

~~~

To visit Paris is to relive a memory, a previous visit not required.

~~~

<>< ><>

<><><>

A Stroll on the Champs

There is an instant nostalgia you feel as a couple in Paris. The words from *Casablanca,* "We will always have Paris" shed their campy familiarity and become fresh and personal. The illusion builds as you stroll up the Champs Elysees toward the Arc de Triomphe. Th avenue seems endless; the Arc looms in a blue haze, seeming always in the far distance. You move as if in slow motion, the focus of some hidden camera, other strollers just figures in a blurred background.

~~~

Paris seemed our private park
For us alone its charm beguiled
For us the Champs stretched to the Arc
For us the Mona Lisa smiled.

~~~

<><><>

<>< ><>

A Visit To The Louvre

At the Louvre, the crowd gathers in a semicircle, roped off to a distance of about thirty feet from Da Vinci's masterpiece. People jostle to get to the front, so as to turn to a friend's camera and get a photo of themselves with the Mona Lisa in the background. If you stand off a bit and take in this scene, the Mona Lisa seems to look past the crowd, her eye catching yours, her enigmatic smile intended for you personally.

~~~

I imagine the young Madonna Lisa del Giocondo posing for her famous portrait, and it occurs to her that in all her life to come, whenever she gazes into a looking glass, she will behold the Mona Lisa -- and a strange little smile comes across her face.

~~~

<>< ><>

<><><>

An Afternoon At The Monet Gardens

The autumn glow of Giverny
Shown velvet soft on you and me.
No breeze astir, no gust to sway
The lily pond of Claude Monet.

~~~

We stood at the foot of Monet's lily pond, looking across at the Japanese foot bridge. I glanced from the actual scene to the Monet print in my hand. It seemed, as I compared the impression to the reality, that Mother Nature had not quite captured it. I realized then that I had long ago fashioned from Monet's impression my own imagined reality, and it had little to do with the lily pond at Giverny.

~~~

The artist gazes upon a reality and creates his own impression. The viewer gazes upon the impression and creates his own reality.

<><><>

<><><>

A Writer's Reverie

And Satan said to the Lord, "I could make you Hemingway in Paris in the 1920's." And the Lord said, "Get away, Satan, for you shall not tempt the Lord thy God."

~~~

We are seated at a sidewalk cafe in Saint Germain, my bride with her cafe noir, I with my schooner of Leffe beer. It is easy enough to fancy that I am the young Hemingway in 1925, at work on *The Sun Also Rises*. Perhaps, this day, the writing has gone well, the sentences honest and true. We sit happily. It is a good time between us and we do not speak. It is good to sit and listen to the noise of the street. The beer is fresh and good and I finish it with pleasure. A few raindrops patter on the cafe awning. We get up and walk back to the hotel in the rain.

~~~

<><><>

<><><>

Meet the Author
Robert Brault

In 1961, while in college, I sold a Picturesque Speech item to Reader's Digest. So began an avocation that has extended to this day. For the next thirty years, I programmed computers for a living and wrote aphorisms for pleasure. Some 1200 made their way into magazines and newspapers between 1961 and 1994.

In 2009, seven years into retirement, and after a fifteen-year recess from writing, I launched an internet blog called *A Robert Brault Reader*. My hope was to find a new audience for my published writings. To my surprise, the effort reawakened the old muse and new thoughts began to flow.

The blog was noticed by Terri Guillemets at *The Quote Garden*, a popular internet quote site. She soon was showcasing some 400 of my items, each with a hyperlink back to my site. Soon thereafter, a Google search would routinely turn up a million sites quoting my items.

It is now twelve years and five books later. Some 2400 copies of the previous four books have sold on Amazon. Hopefully, a tolerant readership will abide one more.

<><><>

<>< ><>

Meet The Artist
Joan Brault

I started painting in watercolors in the mid-1970's at the Connecticut School of Fine Art under Carl Paternostro. I've studied since with other established artists in watercolor, oils and pastels. I am a long-time member of the Avon Arts Association, having served as President, and hold membership also in the Connecticut Pastel Society.

Over the years I've been juried into many Connecticut art shows, including the West Hartford Artwalk, the Connecticut Watercolor Society, the New Hartford Art League, the Golden Thread Society, the Canton Gallery on the Green and have been an award winner in the Granby Land Trust Show. My watercolor was displayed on the cover of The Hartford Courant's I-Towns section, and I was a finalist in their "featured artist" contest.

A continuing activity (and pleasure) in my artistic life is to produce notecards and a yearly calendar combining my artwork with my husband's original quotes. I have also teamed with him to provide the cover art for his book collections. We both hope that you enjoy the selections made for *Thoughts on Art and Artists*.

<>< ><>

"Erie Canal" - pastel by Joan Brault

Made in the USA
Middletown, DE
24 June 2021